Anonymous Intruder

ANONYMOUS INTRUDER

Ian Seed

Shearsman Books
Exeter

Published in the United Kingdom in 2009 by
Shearsman Books Ltd
58 Velwell Road
Exeter EX4 4LD

www.shearsman.com

ISBN 978-1-84861-028-6
First Edition

Acknowledgments
These poems first appeared in or are due to appear in the
following magazines and anthologies: *The Argotist Online, Aught,
Combustible Edge* (a Bluechrome anthology), *The Café Irreal, Dusie,
Exultations&Difficulties, Free Verse, Great Works, Green Integer Review,
Innovative Poetry in English 2005–6* (Green Integer Books), *Litter,
Maquette Magazine, Milk Magazine, nthposition, The Penniless Press,
Poetry Nottingham, Poetry Salzburg Review, Skald, Stride,* and
Wandering Dog.

'At Rest' and 'Not Enough to be Innocent' borrow and mix phrases
from *Le Voleur de Talan* by Pierre Reverdy.

Cover illustration copyright © John Woodcock, 2008.

CONTENTS

3 — Shadows

'It's funny when you become aware of your heart it's as though you can feel it beating in the sky and in nearly everything except yourself really'

— Kenneth Patchen

For J.

1

REARRANGEMENTS

THE FAMILIAR DEAD

1

Transfigured already without
my noticing, the spaces
between the notes are no longer

lonely foreigners lurking
among orthodox ranks of people
along the thoroughfare's

busy length, but a movement
exact and entire as the widening
of your smile. This is scarcely news

yet I swerve speechless, without
a plan, bareheaded in the sun,
looking for a thing to love.

2

City ghosts shift ground,
eyes black with the mirth
of street children. You cannot quite

recognise the darkened version
of yourself in the window. Winding
streets have brought you here

and now you have forgotten
the way home. You sob
like a child to be allowed in.

Your shoulders merge with the canal
at your back. The familiar
dead refuse to leave.

3

You show me the lavish scrapbook
of your life: the journey to school,
the pain of being teased

or shut out in the playground,
the different roads you later took
which in the story

are still your kingdom.
Although your remaining chances
are few, you're leaving again

to trace long shadows back
to their vital source. Among the wreckage
you stay afloat without noticing.

4

The rain was the same in each city.
In my quest for comfort, I'd drained
my journey of all meaning.

Further down the street she asked
if I was a stranger. She'd mistaken me
for someone else. For 50 bucks

she offered a fleeting realm
of scent and warmth. At first
I was afraid to follow. I remember

her goose-pimpled skin, the stocking
with holes, the scattering
of dead matches by the bed.

5

In the hotel room by the railway line
a breeze blew the curtains inward,
shifting fragments of sky.

You lay on your stomach, head pressed
into the pillow, your dress bunched
over your thighs. Afterwards

we went through endless back streets
in search of what was missing.
The summer rain steamed.

You grew tearful at the barefooted
children who dropped stones
into the bowl of a blind man.

6

Concentrate on the architecture,
not the illness, things to make
and mend. Yet it's difficult

to know where you are when
the concision of guides only adds
to the feeling of lostness.

You cannot or will not go
home. For almost every
corner or porticoed street

there's a journey through thick
grey air, a face without
a name at the end of it.

7

On the crowded tram, the accidental
touch of a hand is enough
to pinpoint your loneliness.

You grow open at the mouth,
the city an endless thread
you cannot stop unravelling.

Shadows on the street are pared
away. Each face becomes
beautiful and impossible

seen through a moving window
like dolls waving bright
paper flowers and flags.

Rearrangement

When I become aware of the nakedness of the place, I
hear someone laughing who is really in pain. Approaching
from the other side, I recognise the tangle of lives without
understanding the direction they've come from. My mouth is
trained to form sounds as if I were expressing my own desires,
my body to move as if there had never been another way of
moving. For how could I be caught otherwise between pain
and its expression? Yet I once dreamt of these scenes differently,
without melting away, or wondering who it was they thought
of when they called my name.

Two Old Heads

So, nothing: this, the view shifted,
my mother swimming away,
and the gift of you bending over
in a scene I dreamt of once before,
sudden formlessness raised around you,
too high for you to climb, a voice
lost as I enter the city without you.

But why *these* houses, the sadness of them?
I won't tell you of the impression your shout
makes in the dark. *E poi basta*—
it's enough for you to have knelt down
in the place where you did, only a few moments
ago. To stay upright is tiring—
you should know a few things about that.

Meanwhile the days pass. It's snowy
and foggy. If your father is an executioner,
his face all lit up, how do you translate this
into family terms? I reach out to you
from forgotten wounds, I tell myself words
I have never understood. At times
some dead thing overcomes me. You

or who? The surprise at finding myself
uncomposed in front of an open window,
your promise to close your eyes next time.
No one can tear you away. Did you know
I would grow tired of waiting before you
grew tired of watching? I've tried to understand
what you're telling me and even to tell it

to others who have no objection
to this gift from a lost one. The things
you dream up to make yourself interesting:
'My wife, Anna, is very blond and knows how to dress.'
E poi basta—I'm locking the house and leaving.
The sky is no different from the colour of stone.
What makes me love you makes me want to run.

MODULATED SUBTONES

This wanderer is lacking in all finality.
He'd like to be awake from this moment on, bearing away
the totality of dreams from sleep. Nothing can equal
his days for endlessness, but I can easily believe

you don't find them amusing. A unique chance
presents itself before he leaves. Either way
he'll think all the time of where he isn't, but the air
is good and he can hear donkey bells on the slope.

When he opens the door, it's for us to go away.
We walk along the stream, happy to think of nothing.
It was solitude which brought us together. Here in the village
a boy always buys a girl an ice cream.

I am both speaker and the one spoken to. It's time
for a wonderful lie: 'conversation is sweeter
at night,' 'a dead branch is made more beautiful
by the complicated foliage surrounding it,' 'the exact

proportion of your person is impossible to share.'
I find my friend again—his eyes are no longer used to me.
He covers his mouth with his hand and measures the distance
separating me from myself. I listen to him, seated

on the side of the road. I do not doubt my existence,
nor do I doubt it's personal. I repeat his questions,
turn them over as if they were dusty jewels in my hands,
look away at the thin line separating earth from sky.

WHAT WAS ALIVE

My father's ghost dissolves
into a green morning and bloody evening,
the playfulness of childhood
interlaced with a bent forefinger.

You never asked me about the past,
the forgotten land of my own body.
Though the figure is still close,
the boy's face is mute and blurred.

How seldom a stranger enters.
It was someone else I was calling
who walks away in twilight
without reaching the beginning or end.

The air of the village is undisturbed
where no one has travelled for years,
where exile has taken hold of me
and an unfamiliar language.

TEMPORAL FIX

Little by little I open my eyes in dress suit and white tie.
The office is one thing, home another, what others see
and touch, a face wandering in the garden
among tall flowers and a bit of sky

If I wrote a book called *the world as I found it*,
I would have to include my own body, yet in real life
a proposition is never what we want, only a picture
laid against reality, a measure we make ourselves understand.

We discover to our horror that we don't really believe
in anything at all, people seem to have only outsides.
The erotic lover and his behind do not take pleasure
in the same things. That poor body of mine suffers

an injustice which is not voluntary, but the rejection
of identity removes one method of speaking.
I have never witnessed anyone do their work as diligently
as the corpulent man, red in colour, with two faces,

heart covered in a piece of cloth, like a fire covered
by smoke or a mirror by dust. It is the man who abandons
the result of his actions, passing through many births,
yet no one exists without acting. When he turns pale

I start to cry. Some people get more of the royal
jelly than others, yet out of sixty perhaps
so many who have been to the other side
have nothing to say when they return.

It begins with a crime, the killing of old authorities,
the touch of a lover who cannot look you in the face.
If you're scared of the dark, bring a mask.
It's just too black to see that flower.

BEYOND YOUR CONCERN

Perhaps I travel from body to body
simply to postpone the moment we must meet.
I read the story but never come across your face.

She invites me in with a smile both anxious and pleased.
Will I fit in? Will any of her coterie want to sleep with me?
The sun creates ruby from rock. Our attention is turned

as if through a veil or a kindled flame.
There are many texts but which will you handle first?
The point is surely to begin, nothing else.

While she cuts my hair, she leans her belt buckle into my shoulder.
Coming to this means another possibility altogether:
feeling dizzy and closing my eyes.

Perhaps it's as much as anyone can offer.
She had supper with us that night and her son came to the table.
We don't know if they'll return.

The play is not without risk or love. 'The good which I want to do
I fail to do.' When you brush against me
the story breaks and heals us at the same time.

You have a double face.
Its no use thinking they will save us.
The boy on the corner holds out his hand.

If you were to ask, it would be more than you can think of:
I without myself, you without yourself.
Who will bring us home?

Seemingly Hesitating

I wanted to go further, but couldn't.
A door opened.

The pair I hardly knew—
Could we visit you in Italy this spring?

At first I thought the room was empty
but then I sensed someone else was in there

a woman or a child perhaps.
Never had I known such warmth.

And waited, not wanting the moment to pass.
To accept that you are accepted.

The wide mark of a river
faded frescoes in the village no one visits anymore,

unknowable thoughts of a girl
who smiles with broken teeth:

finding the thread in another language
nothing resolved, everything enriched.

ANXIOUS TRADE

1

Sitting by the road
he too was once a child

I came to another piece of his life
cool shadow the only place

You responded too quickly
in your need for approval

The loneliness of others
the train at the country station

after nightfall distant voices singing
no one for miles around

Resonance grows from consent to emptiness
retreat an act of association

dust rising and falling.

2

It's okay I want it
placing my hand between her thighs

the business of walking
never to stop

hands trailing the darkness
the house abandoned no longer real

How you would love to have your feet on the ground again
It will not disappear so easily

however much you turn away
If it is theirs it is also yours

to love with intelligence not power
Reluctant to unpack when she reached the hotel room

 to commit herself to the idea of staying.

A Kind of Dying

Struggle to attain
weaving
waves of America
from the landing
I saw you
a little light
leading to
a mattress
stained carpet
narrow window
I didn't mean to
the walk by the bookstalls on the quay
not coming up to
you set store by
the street
could lose it
unknowingly
again and again
not how in dreams
a hundred ways the
finding

Anonymous Intruder

1

Don't be surprised if you find yourself bleeding on the road
no thought of reaching the city any more

I am no longer useful to you, not even to myself
standing on the spot where you once begged

It's as if I can still catch the scent of your sweat,
coloured glass smashed at my feet

If I take one piece, I'll see a fragment of your face
I've let go of your hand because I wish to be alone

Further down the hill, we're no longer in the sun
At no moment are we safe from ourselves

It's only a question of crossing the street
You will not be refused

yet when the gift is offered with open hands
it's no longer this you desire

2

Someone peeps into the dark room
the coat hanger still sways in the wardrobe

When I meet her to discuss plans for the conference
I remember how I pictured her the night before

skinny arse up in the air
heavy breasts swinging with each thrust

This fragment is a way to the infinite that I claim as mine
together with all those who crowd in here

The street is not the same as the one you walked yesterday
nor the corner I watched you turning

When you speak another voice is lost
the author of the gesture gone

Your heart charts its own way unseen
Unclothed you kiss the stranger as anyone might

3

At the roadside the body covered by a sheet,
just a few strands of hair in the breeze

brightness in the waving field
Can something so beautiful really burn

The riches you once knew with your finger tips
your own flesh and blood

We're obsessed by the story we will never tell
In your memory the buildings of the city

are much whiter than they really are
limbs of trees stretch over frozen water

You touch me in your dream
I can't read the fading name

on the still-sealed envelope
If only you would turn your face towards me

CHECK OUT GIRLS

1

Tracing a direct line of descent
to scratchy, aging prints, the model
needs to be changed, executed

with precision. Until last year
another burial area, priests at three
churches, they too exact

in all their mannerisms. We have seen
blood and cuts cruelly quoted,
the pink neon sign

flashing 'sexy' in the dining room,
the labelling of the clock on Sunday,
an icy proposal to get ready.

2

The sale of sheep bones represents a profit
and an outcry of gulls on the cliff top.
Would you like seaweed with that?

The decision today deals with serious
beauty without rules, a woman falling
asleep after a bitter tasting meal.

Next week plastic figures with stable
feet and heads will have occupied
the top posts. The trial will be in progress,

beyond that wolves bold enough
to follow brother and father back to
their cottage through blossom-covered apple trees.

3

It'll be very quiet when you girls go.
This young one can accept the idea
of killing herself and other people

but not the idea of sleeping with an instrument
that's worked perfectly for centuries.
You may have had a good life

but there's a real chance of dying in distress.
She got off to a more promising start
on Monday, putting up her first

'Wanted' post, waving from the other side
of the fence, not daring to blink
in case she missed something big.

4

My fragile son surprisingly turned up
on time. I was in the middle
of hanging out curtains.

He loved me, but he loved someone else more,
a song in his head thanks to the lodger
in the spare room.

We embraced before he left.
I shouted 'weetabix' after him
although I don't like

transgressive urges, people
who smell of bombing and gassing,
unrecognizable on a summer's day.

5

Still unsigned in the end
it's so embarrassing it makes me
shut up shop in February.

We've plenty of good stories,
but no voice or believable plan
to grow up or shed light.

Last week, almost every day
the poorly equipped professor
drained his bladder in a separate bed.

Where's the harm, she said,
in emotional foreplay, a necklace
just to look at, a perfect excuse?

6

Recklessness in the air. It's not just
sharply-pointed gentlemen at dawn
or the serious absence

of shopkeepers and good red wine
but the innocent industry of graded
fireflies *sans fin*.

I grow warmer on the bus
travelling along the bumpy road
most noticeably between

stories of apparent smoothness
fashioned from the big book with a twist
of lips, fur and peeling away.

7

At first no one recognises
the tiny French woman with tousled honey hair
striding down to the quay in the rain.

'Once in a street I saw a very old
German soldier, his uniform torn away,
being beaten to death by a crowd.'

The last time she was surrounded
by children playing. Hopes rise
at her broken approach. The heart

doesn't have any nerves of its own.
This is the first awakening, power
coming home in the shadows.

8

Already she knows a lot of people in the city,
cut loose has the feeling she's going to do more
than carry a pair of scissors

in unassembled moments. Turning in her seat
she sees him walk towards her as if
she were a pictureless book,

tapping his little stick, handsome
and unwashed. 'The most difficult thing
about getting here is the smell

which changes all the time.'
When she looks into his eyes, all she sees
are tiny reflections of herself.

9

I had been at a loss to know
how to deal with my fringe.
Dust the tart with icing sugar in the best

possible sense of that word.
A series of posters now advertises
'Miss Sixty' at Milan tram stops.

We wanted to show what it was like
at the end of a long voyage
through enticingly broken structures

when you see the same faces
selling poppies from a tray
and singing songs you know backwards.

NOTICES

1

around the corner a pang
half wanted that sweet crawl
but cut to hoisting red
the first packet of nerves
kingly and hesitant beside
the culled horse a mask
further catered so far
a graft shape so fabulous
gatherer of signs

2

from shape of sails
desires a story but first
lock the breeze for pretty
much its link passes
or burns newly broken
a friend north with fingers
whose face beside the text
dreams the melt of the other
with smoke and heal

3

yet changed even
riskier lacks a single
or shades inhabit blocks
compositional though unreal
yes you can have me
depart and unfold loose
patch yet chance
had both a packet of light
warmth our god

4

whose roots deep figure
at times who persist
picture to grow space
depict joy whitened
or unfold their utterly
constructed strangers still
more remarkably plots
blesséd I feel
history of the sweet

5

was the smell published
keep asking my pitch
black a tale of kinder
or promise made to measure
since science and religion
sell body you are
colour to take forehead
and deep wander this blur
on the brink of town

6

angels between irony
indeed sometimes a mouth
of carbon ways returns
the right to wear yet
if the product is so good
why the hard sell otherwise
the last one contains
grades of vertical children
to reflect the beginning

7

transit from distance or deep
melt said couldn't he stay
still about the time
meaning the last course
passer by I love you
what are you doing avid
father the same year
mining barracks blue
stains the scene or near
divide emerges

8

escape as simply remain
taught wings to pair
in rain how I paint
colour or pause the difference
this is the entrance
undertake at best
broken or else a river
endear with cut bodies
more than night leaves

9

bending seems the first
string of barely illicit
themselves blue city
start tremendous eyes
only flow a moment draw
what you have built
yet capture the stem
of unmistakeable face
to signal it's better

FROM A LONG WAY

Sometimes I asked: how do I reach
this truth? Each time I was surprised
by the pictures they painted of you
as if day or night could be framed.

So I stepped out and journeyed
not to learn your secrets but to see you
tying your shoe laces beside the path
which cuts into the mountain as it climbs.

2

VOICES

Recount

The first green. Crows squawk away from treetops. In the river, a replica of the branches we walk under, but colder, without colour. A dog wanders, indifferent to rain. You question that 'finally' once more, the husk of our lives swept away by one casual encounter too many. Wine on the terrace. I've been dreading the moment, too terrified to turn, but they are all smiling, glad to see us. What has changed is hardly perceptible. The work is ours.

WITNESS

The plot is afoot, though nothing obvious observed. It's not right, she said, tight-lipped, standing in the queue for tickets. Turn left at the end of the building. Dreams would arrive and not be dealt with on an immediate basis. Don't assume the trick is to wake with a start in the middle of the night. Red rimmed eyes, suddenly old, the plot not what he thought it was. He could have taken a different road, but the resulting fragment would not of necessity been any further away from scissored nerves. I know it's only longing that makes you turn away.

BROKEN WINDOW

Just one ritual. She cries in the morning when she wakes. We can benefit from the direction of the other, according to an unwritten law that exists solely for the sake of bursting into song. Just the burden of the thought that breathless work is possible, after all, at the end of a day of grey hours. Yet the anxiety is still there in her eyes that he will make fools of them both, waiting to make conversation with the stranger at the bar, less cunning than before. I stop to look through locked iron gates into the empty park at dusk. It turns out the bastard was right. We were free, but it was an empty freedom, like wandering in and out of abandoned houses at will.

Mine Before Night

Come to the trick of avoiding touch, wandering through Sunday
afternoon crowds by the river Po, obliged to come to a sticky
end. Sudden warmth under the sheets, skin against skin, afraid
for a moment she would repulse him. Power could not reside
all in one room, whatever their illusions. There is another circle,
unseen, behind this one. A shirt takes the shape of the chair
it hangs on, the time of vacancy where we worship winners.
Granted, but what can replace the heat of your hands, playful at
the crucial moment? Roles crumble, delve to a deeper set.

All Kinds of Dust

Music was our first love, but there was little time for that. For
years we assembled our ideas cautiously as we travelled from
land to land, compiling our survey. One day we were drawn to
a tavern by the sound of singing. A fatal error. The tune of the
gipsy fiddle gave us glimpses of a reality we had long buried
deep beneath the surface. All kinds of dead people came to
life, an old skull, lain long in the snow, abandoned in search of
something more exotic and otherworldly, whatever could be
lifted and turned slowly to reflect the light coming from the
next room. A fat man smiled behind the counter, shelves of
impossibly coloured bottles just an arm's reach away. A girl with
a dark wing of hair across her temple approached our table.

CONSEQUENCES

A stone dislodged, running through grey light, the clatter of
an unseen train to our left. We stop at the edge of the forest.
I can still see us, strolling down the main thoroughfare of
the pink town by the sea, latticed sunlight across our faces,
winter forgotten. Such kids then, spirited out of the business
up north, as if a promise were for a lifetime. Now afraid to
negotiate beyond the sound of our own breathing in the dark.

The Gift

Exposed at three in the morning, the supposed millennium.
Affection for tables and chairs might be of more use, not born
of desire. The office was another place altogether, murder just
on the other side of his smile. Even the girl singing in the
toilet couldn't be trusted. No holds barred to account for
deeds of other times, tearing at the throat like thirst, walking
down the corridor, afraid of fainting, unready for an upbeat
version of the world, when the wonder of it has a magic
desperation, nothing decided, much freedom still to ride from
one day to another. It could be argued in many ways, all kinds
of desertions endlessly discussed, taking us away from what is
important. Then why am I so cold when you approach, afraid
of what you hold in your hands, closed over your belly?

I That Was Near Your Heart

All the faces gone. Is it this you wanted? The whispered words
you can't catch, the business of angels pressing near you? And
the whirl of a face, Christ bent to a new position, truth without
a dwelling. Still she moans in her sleep, holds your hand to her
belly, anointed in a deed unplanned. All sides lose credence, the
old ritual dried at source, malleable for the first time in defeat.
But a sense of it strikes for the first time. Fingers delicately
intervene. The look in a cow's eyes as she drinks from the river
at dusk. Only a few miles from home.

MARCH

Trees still dead. Gulls looking for pickings in fields of frozen mud. Just before she went to sleep she thought of the buses gathered in the station across the street, 'resting for the night'. That was eighteen years ago, when the roads were covered by a different skin. Nothing came of touching you. Those at a distance could see the picture being built. A hand settled on your wrist and squeezed. It was your voice, but someone else speaking from the side of your mouth.

From Nowhere

Wet with rain she arrived at the door after everyone had gone
to bed. I let her in, knowing she was lost, and told nobody.
Was I fifteen at the time? A restlessness keeps me moving, not
wanting to come to the end of the story. Her cough kept me
awake most of the night. Life melts away like a fable, leading
to another dimension. Easier to have heartstrings tugged by
the next stranger than to heal the situation as it is. I'm not
tired, she said. The one great book was a star which put us to
sleep and woke us at the same time. No one recognised the
two ragged figures emerging from the wood. I remember
now how her eyes closed.

3

SHADOWS

ATTITUDES

We button up our collars and coats. A woman stares out from behind a curtain. Attitudes have hardened. You stutter at the crucial moment, the frame of a dead language pressed over your tongue. There is still a possibility to draw back, assume a role in order to survive. Faith steers shy, nourishes itself, like a heart, in darkness. All kinds of trivia enter the story: your cough in the empty street, a stone in your shoe as we reach the edge of the city. The tale unfolds, a far cry from what we expected.

THE ONLY ONE AWAKE

You talk to yourself out loud, like your father in his youth, a mark of recognition, a baptism. How will you get in touch now? It is already morning yet still dark. You listen to the crackle of rain from your bed. Your hand reaches into the emptiness. You have just come to an understanding. A little time more and it will be done. We walk through the forest in silence, as if the other did not exist, the right way a nomad's journey.

Having Just Breathed

The night bus pulls out of the empty station. You turn pages, twisting a strand of hair around your finger, wanting never to reach the end. Details resist the temptation of the perfect statue, wonderful and terrifying at the same time. Headlights catch a girl, head down, walking along the edge of the road. Your call is unheard. The city disappears street by street as you enter it. You will come to know him without ever seeing his face.

SHADOWS

Brushing the dust from your clothes, you make your way into the town, as if it has been waiting for you all your life, but the town knows nothing of your existence, even after you have spent years wandering its streets. Footsteps clump past your tiny room each night. The same door slams shut at the end of the corridor. Someone calls your name. The voice is always behind you, no matter how many times you turn around.

RECOGNITION

Eri andato via, only years later to understand its true value, always searching for another voyage to return from, coming out of the plot into the wilderness. A nonsense defined you. In different cities, you followed her up never-ending stairways, later to emerge no wiser, but older and changed. Wrapped like a parcel, you were sent on your way for a few pennies. The laughter of Italian children reached you sitting on a broken wall, your face raised to winter, a prayer whispered in your bones.

Shadow of Blade

It was curiosity brought me to the garden wall. You are not here to greet me. There are shouts from the house about an intruder, not for the first time a danger of never entering the scene, only the merest of glimpses, as you climb steep steps in the dark to where music is playing. What do you hope to find there? This is a death which is new to us.

BETRAYAL

Lost in the wet mist, I met a hermit who led me to his hut.
The hut was bare, just two stone benches. He wanted me to lie
down and sleep, though I hadn't eaten all day. 'Tomorrow we
shall find food,' he promised, and held my hand to comfort me.
I dreamt of crows flying, blood dripping like rain from their
beaks. When I awoke, there was a hole in my throat, into which
I was able to insert a finger.

Red Glow

You have one thought above all others, still an air of cheekiness about you, perhaps your only saving grace at this midpoint in your life. Easy to lose, persuaded of the importance of one's role. The hotel was not what I expected. There were shouts from one room to another in a language I couldn't understand. It was too late to go anywhere else. At first light, I met the American in the lobby as arranged. The money he offered for the job was good. He told me he trusted me, assured me no one would come to any harm. I was transfixed by the red glow of his cigarette. When I shook hands with him, it was like being penetrated. Never had I felt so alone.

White Sun

Fingers tapped, perusing products. A whirring fan did little
to keep the place cool. Simple diagrams in an ancient book
illustrated the secrets of the universe, but I seemed to have
forgotten your name as we stepped out into the street. It was
time perhaps to start again, dig out last coins and drop them
into the held out hat on the corner. The waiting boat was full
to the brim, stuff gathered over the years. We could only speak
in broken sounds that no one understood.

Authentic Life

Not the name, but the walk down to the river, a wish
unspoken. In place of a flowchart, a tapestry rolls down before
uncomprehending workers. In this room you are suddenly older.
Something you're afraid to speak of. Bleeding from the nose at
the moment you arrive. So many true versions of the same thing.
Drinking from a tap whose water tastes of rust.

Long Buried

On the bus the warmth of her thigh against mine when I was eight. Seeing these streets for the first time. Her breath on the back of my neck to be believed or discarded. Where footsteps fall silent, the meaning still in the movement of your hand. It wasn't all plain sailing, she said, on the back of something else, not real but enough to keep pace with us through the city. The wearisome old man insists on telling us his tale. But perhaps it is someone else calling, long buried. That was a name, red as the flesh you dreamt of.

At Rest

Without knowing where the singing comes from, they stop on the pavement to listen. But someone else is watching. You can see nothing and know everything, trying to remember where she went. Every one is waiting for the train to depart, a pretty face at the window. The past we created doesn't die, though the house seems empty. Between two barriers you can see the street. We always leave something at the door, which opens without anyone noticing. The sound of rain imitates footsteps.

Not Enough to be Innocent

We gave him back his melted wings. Everyone wanted to see him, but he didn't dare to raise his head. He almost wanted to laugh. Young, he felt old. Five o'clock at the station, not knowing where to rest. Extend arms lighter than mist. Through the hole in the ground another world exactly the same as this one. Faces in the mirror looking. No one knew how to watch over your memory.

A Cry Permitted

From a handful of bones we created a story. There's a constant
sense of alarm, swirling faces, jeans tight around fat bottoms.
Promoted within a year. That's a career with prospects while the
song remains unheard. Drink coffee from a paper cup, sitting
in a smaller and smaller corner, still the childlike searching in
your eyes for something beyond proximal and distal powers, no
pattern discerned, though occasionally scattered words begin a
new language, a nudge in the right direction. Inside the plastic
bag at the counter, a live heart is beating. There is nothing you
need to understand. Shake hands and surrender to another
vision. Ashes were born from less. A man digs into his back
pocket to see if he can find the right coins.

ENCODING

The hand moves away, contemplating the end of the tunnel,
abandoning the page in a hotel room. No time but dust on
water in a glass, the imperfection of paradise, to be cut where
cut is possible. The difference resides in feasibility, rife with
forgetfulness, swept away knowledge. The blue of the eyes
sharpened by a thick dark beard is strangely familiar. It doesn't
have to be like that. The insight disappears on waking. Persistent
otherwise, the room is renumbered, a cave of hair around him.
And that one there, when you were another, pale brown light,
ash down to where you could be forgiven. Nothing to be
renamed in spite of this, nothing outside the room.

DWELLING

Pinched between finger and thumb, the wind builds its own tunnel. The view from the house has gone, the wire along which voices sing. Rain on the back of your hand, you step down onto the empty platform stretched out like a bone. This is just the beginning. Yet how many years did it take you to arrive at this point? The stranger with palms outstretched in the next doorway has infinite knowledge not put to use. It doesn't matter how badly. He hardly feels your touch.

CHARITY

You pick up where the thread left off, enter a landscape the people around you are too busy to see. Time to reclaim, if it is a question of reclaiming at all. What does 'fond of' mean in this context, where you are dazzled by sunlight? They appear from nowhere, pieces of a puzzle that won't fit, but beautiful as fragments. It would be a mistake to wait at this point. You have to go on, try to reach 100, a destiny that would weigh on your conscience if you hadn't slipped around the corner into the next street.

ALMOST

Only one island among others. Beyond the thin stream, where footprints vanished, nobody noticed you waiting, particularly at night. The string of notes was bent to your desire, dancing just below the surface, marking your progress, although at that time invisible. I leaned over your lips. It seemed an odd miracle that my feet were moving, taking me from one side of the road to the other.

Lightning Source UK Ltd.
Milton Keynes UK
22 February 2011

167978UK00001B/20/P